SHE DID

SINGLE

PARENTING

IN HEELS

24 Simple, Straight to The Point Strategies for Being A Kick-Ass Mom

SHE DID

SINGLE

PARENTING

IN HEELS

Kids Grow Up Too Fast

Author

Latiqua Williams

All scripture quotations, are taken from the KING JAMES VERSION. KJV. Public Domain

For information about special discounts for bulk purchase, contact the author @infosinglemom@gmail.com

D.O.R.M. International Publishing

Visit our website at www.divine-order.org

Printed in the United States of America

First Edition: August 2018

10 9 8 7 6 5 4 3 2 1

Library of Congress Cataloging-in-Publication Data

Latiqua Williams

She Did Single Parenting in Heels / Latiqua Williams – 1st ed.

ISBN-13: 978-0-9862493-9-6

ISBN-10: 0-9862493-9-4

D.O.R.M
PUBLISHING

Dedication

Kick-Ass Single Mom

I dedicate this book to my loving sons Michael, J'nie, and Randy; and to my beloved maternal grandmother, Avis Williams. I am honored to be your granddaughter and

I hope you are smiling down on me in heaven.

My life was no accident. God instructed me to be your mother before the womb. You boys have given me my why.   Teaching me that my trials in life and the unfortunate situations have built a strong woman Through it all, my faith has not wavered.

BUT GOD HAD HIS PLAN FOR MY LIFE.
Imperfect, Yet Loved by GOD... Imperfectly
perfect!

In this journey, I have learned that my trials are my
testimony to the world. Sons, you have taught your
mother how to SMASH FEAR in the face, walk boldly
past pain, and positioned me to step into forgiveness,
push past the struggles and faithfully walk into my
purpose. With my heels on! Unapologetically! NO matter
if my heels were purchased at Wally World, Rainbows,
Goodwill or those "Red Bottoms that hurt my damn
pinky toe.

All three of you have throned me with a crown that can
never be taken off.

**A BOLD, FAITH-FILLED, FEARLESS MOTHER,
who is breaking the STEREOTYPE of SINGLE
PARENTING!**

" A Successful Woman is one who can build a firm
foundation with the bricks others have thrown at her."

P.O.W.E.R...

People Overcoming Weakness Everyday Relentlessly.

TABLE OF CONTENTS

I AM LOVED…

John 3:16

Introduction

Every child needs a powerful mother in their life.

An enthusiastic mother, a loving smile that spreads throughout an entire room.

A Praying mother that will continue praying for her children to go in the right direction in life.

We all have the potential to be great mothers, and we have the opportunity every day to boost our family onward and upward.

Our job is a highly influential one with no instructions, no hiring packet and no probation period.

Unfortunately, in the day to day struggles of single motherhood, our good intentions can easily slip away from us and fly out the window.

You had the right plans for your life, but somewhere along the way, this SINGLE MOTHER position had an opening and slid right on in and applied to your life without you even asking for it. You are now the _CEO of SINGLE PARENTING_. (Oh, and hey, also the manager, doctor, dad, tooth fairy, administrative assistant, counselor, janitor, chef, bus driver, coach and the bank)...

You get my drift!

But heck, you look around and think Oh Hell Naw.

The Devil is Liar" You mean to tell me we don't get the house with the husband, 2.5 children with the white picket fence and the dog?!?

After all, that's the American Dream, isn't it

You don't get the opportunity to go on special vacation excursions with your girls and laugh till you piss your pants, and drink wine.

Bye Felicia, your life has changed

This book is written to help single parenting mothers conquer their challenges in adjusting to life and raising a kick-ass family your way!

Yes, the expectations, purpose and the possibility we all felt in the beginning, even in the midst of everyday struggles of raising your family.

Today I want to share with you my 24 Straight To The Point Strategies to raising a family and being a KICK ASS MOM **UNAPOLOGETICALLY** ......

Kick-Ass Single Mom Starting Today

7 Things to Stop

Kick Ass Single Mom Starting today 7 Things to Stop!

The Wise Woman Builds Her House.

Proverbs 14:1

Before we get into The 24 Straight To The Point Strategies To Being A Kick Ass Mom,

There are 7 Things you must STOP doing right now before you dive into this book.

1. Stop trying to please everyone!

2. Throw that insecure trash talking woman in your head in the garbage. **KICK HER ASS OUT NOW!**

3. Stop putting yourself down!

4. Stop blaming other people for your mistakes!

5. Stop living in your past!

6. Stop thinking someone will rescue you!

7.   Stop comparing yourself to other women you may see as great mothers!

Never Underestimate the Power of a Single Mother.

Dear Younger You,

I know how you feel. I remember it so clearly. Every Scared Feeling.. Every Emotion… Confused with everything changing..

Younger you take hope in all things will get better..

Don't focus on the trials and heartache as a teen mom.

Focus on God

He has tailor-made you for an incredible life that you can't even imagine..

The Lord loves and cares for you so deeply..

Hold on and believe this daily..

Don' t Quit….

Teen Mom Story ..

Who am I to think that at 16 years old, I had my life all planned. I mean listen, you could not tell me anything. I had outlined every detail of my future life and mapped it out like mapquest.

That is until November 9th, 1993, when my life unraveled into 24 different ways. I quickly became a teenage mother in a blink of an eye.

My planned life changed. All the picture perfection gave me a fictitious sense of control.

You see, I had already had my mind set to travel the world, run a company where I would design clothes, model, create funky hairstyles and drinks lots of wine. Oh, and how could I forget, you can't be a diva without **RED LIPSTICK**! Well, nope! That's not how it turned out.

I was a teenager giving birth to a child.

Honey heck, I was a child myself.

As my friends sat around the lunchroom planning college tours, exchanging boyfriends stories, etc., my mind was raging with diapers and baby formula.

My thoughts were nothing like theirs. Shit, I was still in total shock that a simple visit to the nurse for gas pains turned out to be actual pregnancy pains.

Oh Hell No, was my initial thought.

How so? No not me! We only had sex a few times. Damn that song," I wanna sex you up"!

That's when I quickly began blaming everyone and everything. All types of crap ran through my head. Not taking responsibility for none of my actions.

It was easier to simply blame others.

Come to think of it; I wasn't ready to be a parent.

To be perfectly honest I didn't even know how to have a serious conversation with my linky, all-star basketball player boyfriend to tell him that our high school years were about to become baby years.

Oh, how my life sucked on this day. I went from having to take a shit, to feeling like shit, to shit just got real!!

As I sat in the nurse's office, I was in complete shock. Her mouth was moving, and I did not hear one damn word she was saying. Oh, I heard one thing, "let's call your parents."

NO MA`AM was the response that flew out of my mouth.

You see, the nurse wanted to speak with my mother. She desired to inform her that we were having a baby.

In my head, I had already checked out and ran like Forrest Gump.

My fear was whether my boyfriend was going to stick around so we could tell our moms that we were having a baby or would this be an "alone" conversation that I would have with my mom.

I was sure hoping that I would not have to battle this alone. After all, I didn't make the baby myself, were the thoughts that ran through my mind.

I had the gift to gab at an early age.   I managed to convince the school nurse that we would gather our parents and inform them of the news, and she would do her job by reporting my pregnancy just to our guidance counselors.

Well, that heffa lied to my face! I should have made her pinky promise that she would not disclose our business. Something that was supposed to be kept in confidence quickly spread around the school like wildfire. Damn, you would have thought that I had slept with O.J. Simpson.

By this time, all the questions begin ringing in my head, the who, how's and the what's of motherhood.

As I'm about to leave the nurse's office, there stood my boyfriend at the door with his pearly white teeth showing, holding his basketball.

He was like "what's up? Damn during lunch you were with the nurse? What's wrong?" "Umm, we are pregnant," I blurted out. He dropped his ball, and of course, those pearly white teeth were no longer showing.

Of course, I had to give him a quick jab. Oh, you and your song **"I Wanna Sex You Up"** got me *PREGNANT* is what I then said.

My boyfriend looked at me and said, *"Well, tell your mother I moved to Africa."*

Africa!! What!Boy stop, you ain't going to No damn Africa.

Believe it or not, we both were horrified of our mothers, as we both came from single-parent homes. We both took a deep breath and was like we're in trouble, let's face it. In the back of my head I was thinking she going to make me read for nine months. She already had a requirement of dating her son. Reading and embracing your culture was a few of them.

I instantly felt some relief knowing my boyfriend was going to be by my side. At this time, he informed that he had gotten accepted into college of his choice. He looked at and said before you get all sad, trust me we will get through this, Ms. Williams. Let's just get past this announcement without mothers.

For some reason, the school officials didn't give him much grief. The weirdest thing was I felt more of the negativity every day. From school faculty and students. and the comments where "She planned her pregnancy", Why should she stop him from pursuing a college career? and She is trying to hinder him from living his best life."

That's what happens when you're the high school basketball star.

Nagging thoughts stayed in my head just like an overdue rental from blockbuster.

How would we care for our baby? Who would watch the baby?

The fear of not being good enough crept inside of me, negatives thoughts from my childhood had rented space in my head, now only to have the thoughts of my guidance counselor were stained into my head as well. ***"I would not graduate***. You might as well withdraw from school now and get a GED".

The spirit of defeat, failure and everything else deposited into me like a negative bank account.

You know those **NSFs (NON-SUFFICIENT FUNDS).** At that very moment, I felt like my life was bankrupt. Deposits of defeat were coming by the minute. The school principal looked into my eyes, depositing more defeat and spoke these very words, "Latiqua, your child would not live to see the age of 13". Oh gosh, how I would love for my school official to see my son now, The Real TaRzann.

When I say my soul was weak, I felt the hairs on my back stand up! My 16-year-old self, felt as if the world had turned its back on me on again.

I was dreading to see mother. Not knowing how to present the startling news about my pregnancy. So I did what I only knew at this moment, take a deep breath. Embrace the moment, drowning in a sea of emotions. I quickly walked up to mother where she was styling hair in the salon. She greeted me with love always and was excited to hear about my day at school. Mother had no idea about the bombshell I was about to announce. My heart was beating 90 miles an hours, palms were sweaty, and I felt as if someone was beginning to cut my oxygen off. I took a deep breath, hugged mother and quietly said, My Period is late!! The one and only thing that I could do was run into the bathroom and lock the door. I felt safe for a brief moment as my mother was quiet, which is unusual.

Only to hear her reaction to my teen pregnancy was "it's your bed, you lay in it." You will not go on welfare; you better figure out how you will provide for this child.

I felt as if I was on an emotional roller coaster ride never to be forgotten, drained, and fearing what else may come flying out of mothers mouth.

As I came out of the bathroom, I began to sink deeply into the pit of a negative state of mind. I started to fear what the next person had to say. But strangely, I impatiently waited so I could give them a damn piece of my mind.

There are a handful of people whose opinion I held in high regard, and one of them was my Nana Avis. I listened to her with great respect.

But the rest of my family, teachers, and people in the community, I didn't give a damn what they thought.

In my mind, that self - sabotaging female was saying to me "girl, you are not wise enough. You can't raise a baby. You should just end your life right now. Maybe you should stop giving a damn too."

It was my Nana Avis who saved me from wanting to call it quits.

She said, **"Tiki,** it's up to you how you present your life to the world.

You can tell your story with passion and purpose, or someone else can deliver your life story to the world with a bunch of nonsense and no truth."

Nana Avis had a way with words. Her family values were based on love and commitment. And, she was firm in whatever you set your mind to, you had better Kick-Ass while doing it; that was her mentality.

Giving up in her eyes was not an option. As I think of it now, she is the very reason why I did not let the *self-sabotaging chick that was living in my head win* and were the kick-ass attitude comes from to this day.

Looking at me with so much love in her eyes she said, "you have enough family members that will support you and make sure that you graduate from high school.

You have to be willing to sacrifice and know that you will succeed."

When Nana Avis gave her word, she was firm. She was a woman who raised 11 children on her own and didn't play any games. Nor did she allow society to box her in by applying limiting beliefs to her family.

One of Nana favorite quotes was ***"We don't play no mind games."***

That very day she taught me a valuable lesson at the tender age of 16.

And, it was**, It's all in your Mindset**.

You become what you think.

*** Tiki***, when you bring this baby into this world, you can allow the mind to absorb pain, lack in your basic necessities, live in poverty, and incompleteness.

Or you can let

GOD be your primary source and speak life into your child. Challenge the no's in life.   Place your child in a loving environment. Speak life into this baby and destine him for greatness."

And that's what I did.

Upon giving birth to my child, I took my Nana Avis's advice, and I spoke life into my baby and myself.

Do you know that only 63% of teenage girls who give birth before the age of 18 either graduate from high school with a **GED** or dropout?

To me, that means the remaining 37% have the power to beat the odds! Come on now, I know we all got some **Ass Kicking** in us. I was the teenage mother who was lacking experience, skills maturity, and economic security.   As with all mothers, we all start off not knowing what parenting will bring us.

During my youth, a movie called Fear stayed in my head,

especially after becoming a teenage mother. The film continually played in my mind day in and day out. Fearing what percentile, I would fall into GED, HIGHSCHOOL DROPOUT or DIPLOMA.

Life is what you make it.

Accept what is, let go of what was, and have faith in what will be.

I had faith, and now I had to allow my grandmother's highly influential words to penetrate my heart.   Even though that movie was still playing in my head, and I felt like all the odds were against me.

Guess what I told myself? Forget that! I'm not falling into no box, nor was society going to stigmatize my baby or me for that matter. I had to figure out quickly my purpose and it damn sure was not residing in the projects, trying to hang pictures up on a cement wall and living off of a welfare check for a measly $224.00 a month.

Shit, I was narrowing down to the 52% of mothers on public assistance that had their child as a teenager. Imagine what the other 48% did.

I'll just go ahead and tell you, they decided to defy the odds and beat the statistic!

Well, this was my life for a brief moment.

But, that was not how my story was going to end nor was it my final destination.

I had to shift my mindset and take no prisoners. Somebody was counting on me. The mental game and mental focus was a must for me to survive.

Believe in your potential, not your past.

My LIFE just got REAL.

It was time to become a KICK ASS MOM, AND TAKE LIFE BY THE THROAT.

Oh, and for the record, my high school boyfriend asked me the same damn question every day for nine months, "did your period come today?

REALLY?!

No period! But what I did have was a beautiful, healthy baby boy who changed our lives for the better.

That's just part of the teen mom story… to be continued

Kick-Ass Single Mom 24 Strategies

Be A Woman That Never Gives UP!

No More Collapsing in your Home!!!

I Can Be a Powerful Mother.

I Will Be a Powerful Mother.

I Must Be a Powerful Prayerful Mother.

Single mommas don't carry any news!

Central Focus: What happens in your home, stays in your home.

Affirmation

I Can. I Will.. I must leave all of my family business, life dealings, situations at the door of my home.

Single mommas, thou shall Have 11 Commandments for your life and family.

(I have written the 11 commandments for you to use as a guide.)

Central Focus: Create a doctrine for your family.

Command family values, morale, integrity and financial independence.

Teach your family that you have decided not to be POOR

Affirmation

I now consciously and willingly affirm.

I am a great provider.

I am a great producer.

I am a great giver

I am a great tither

Ask God to reveal your talents so you can produce wealth for your family.

Single mommas throw the victim out of the window.

Central Focus: Single mommas you are responsible for you and your family. You no longer can blame anybody. This includes your ex-boyfriend, your mother, your school officials, boo-boo kitty or your current living situation.

You can no longer play the victim!

You are now the victorious mommas!

Affirmation

I **affirm** to own my life.

I **affirm** not to play the victim game

I **affirm** that I am a Victorious momma

Single mommas know how to deal with the "bonus parents," divorced family, baby mommas, kids nagging nanny or new booboo kitties that are so extra.

<u>**Central Focus:**</u> Single mommas remember you are writing your story over, don't succumb to the damn foolery.

Take responsibility and break the cycle. Provide the absent parent and booboo kitty a cheat sheet.

This sheet has the guidelines for the steps you are willing to take to compromise and reconcile your family differences. You   do everything in your power to facilitate a healthy relationship, and your kids will thank you.

And moms, our job is to accept responsibility for our children's well-being.

Now listen, everyone ain't cut out for a dang on a cheat sheet. So as I said before, you may have to bow out gracefully until the relationship can be based on the child and not the past adult issues.

Ok?!

Mommas are the role models. Don't dangle the child over the absent parent's head.

Don't use the baby as a power tool. Look at your child as the most significant **GIFT** that has happened to you, knowing God knew you were a queen who would get the job done well.

Affirmation:

I affirm that I am imperfectly perfect by GOD.

I affirm that my child is the most significant gift that I have been blessed with!

I affirm that I can do anything that GOD allows me to do!

#5

Single mommas, you and only you determine your family's worth.

Central Focus: Single momma you are your rescue. You are the beautiful mom that says "I will drastically change my family worth. "They say single moms are weak and needy; the devil is Liar Not you!

Single mommas have to be willing to grab life by the throat and believe in the unseen.

Affirmation:

I affirm today that I will turn my struggle into triumphs

I affirm that I have unshakable faith

I affirm that I will create and not complain

I affirm that I will utilize the skills that I already have

Single mommas need to set family boundaries.

Central Focus: This falls in line with self-love. Take responsibility for your happiness. Be honest and up front, focus on what you can control, not what you can't.

If the absent parent checks out from parenting, grab your kids, grab your lipstick and your heels and love on your babies. Get y'all a family song, dance, laugh, and cry with them if you have too.

But don't forget to shower them with love and respect. Teach them how to set boundaries in their lives. THEY MATTER AS WELL.

Affirmations;

I affirm that it's okay to start over

I affirm that my family is rediscovering their life

I affirm to be a courageous momma with boundaries

I affirm to take the time to teach my family about the importance of self-love.

Single mommas do what you feel is the next best move for your Family.

Central Focus: Prioritize, keep an open mind.

Remember you ain't gonna cook dinner every night, so get over it! Shit, a bowl of cereal or a turkey and cheese sandwich standing up in the kitchen, chatting with the family won't make you a bad mom.

Affirmations

I affirm to ditch the perfect momma status

I affirm to laugh, love and live a little

I affirm to appreciate my life daily

Single mommas, please do not try to be your kid's friend.

Central Focus: Plain and simple. And, yes whoopings still exist!. BOOM, just like that!!

Affirmations:

I affirm to discipline in a positive way

I affirm to talk about issues before they are issues

I affirm to the courage to do what's right

#9

Single mommas, there is no such thing as a perfect family or kids.

<u>Central Focus</u>: Live a little and have fun. Bring the family to Costco and have a party. Walk down the aisles take a sample or two; shit take three promo samples. Y'all know Costco is off the chain on Saturday mornings with the excellent cheese and crackers. Go down those aisle dancing and singing "Single Mom Squad. Oh yeah!" in your Lil' John voice. Yeah, yeah.

<u>Affirmations:</u>

I affirm to laugh and be bold

I affirm to smile

I affirm to be radical

Single mommas, you have to be willing to make mistakes as a mother.

(GET YOUR ASS UP! Once you've dusted yourself off, get your lady business waxed. And trust me this hurts like a mutha, this will make you regroup real fast.)

<u>Central Focus</u>: Don't Dwell in your mistakes... Let's Face it our mishaps makes us stronger woman, Mother, Sisters, and daughter...

Thanks to my bestie, this experience made me have superpowers. Shoot, let me stop lying.

That waxing felt so bad I wanted to jump off the table with all of my goods out.

Affirmation

I affirm I will brighten up my spirit and laugh –a – minute as a mother...

I affirm that I am beautiful

I affirm I allow peace in my life

Single mommas, turn your wounds into WISDOM.

Central Focus: Pain is temporary and quitting lasts forever. When it comes to parenting, we may feel tired, frustrated and perhaps feel at times the easiest way is to give up and quit. I get it because I was there too at a point in time of my life. Turning your wounds to wisdom is like turning fear into confidence.

Life experience enhances our wisdom, a skill that you will use your whole life. It builds your confidence, empowering you to move forward.

Affirmations:

I affirm I am braver than I think

I affirm to create healthy, winning habits

I affirm to be grateful every day

Single mommas, stop doing what you want, do what you SHOULD.

Central Focus: If you feel you should have a therapist, well get a therapist. If you think you should dance in the rain, have at it.

Do what makes you smile.

Affirmations:

I affirm to dance for 2mins daily

I affirm to awaken my spirit

I affirm that I will pursue what makes me happy

#13

Single mommas demand respect for yourself and your family.

Central Focus: No matter what your circumstances! Children deserve respect to thrive. You better put some RESPECT on my family name.

Affirmations:

I affirm to respect myself to walk away from anyone that no longer serves me

I affirm to self-discipline

I affirm that my life is important

Single mommas create the life you want in HEELS.

<u>Central Focus:</u> Live life without guilt or shame.

Walk into the life you want, one step at a time with your heels and rock it, baby!

Affirmations:

I affirm to be happy every day

I affirm to live a purpose filled life

I affirm I am Phenomenal

#15

Single mommas kick the "Disease to Please" in the ASS!

<u>**Central Focus**</u>**:** Dare to put those heels on, dare to reprioritize your life. You are rewriting your story, no more pleasing.

(This goes for your ex, the boss, the economy, the church friends, your mothers, or hell your friend who has the so-called perfect man...hmm, he ain't perfect.)

Affirmations:

I affirm to respect myself to walk away from anyone that no longer serves me

I affirm to self-discipline

I affirm that my life is important

Single mommas see the beauty in saying NO!

<u>**Central Focus:**</u> You are just one woman, you are not superwoman, and you can't do everything on your own. So, put your lipstick on, grab your Heels and say NO.. With no explanation!

Affirmations:

I affirm to take daily actions on saying no

I affirm to make myself a priority

I affirm to saying no more often with feeling guilty

Single mommas have a 24-Hour Rule!

<u>**Central Focus:**</u> even with the non-custodial parent or that out of line nosy neighbor. I like to call this the cooling down period. However, if you wake up the next day still feeling angry, you should then express how you feel.

Affirmations:

I affirm to get crystal clear about my feelings

I affirm to give myself time to respond

I affirm to write a note of all things that frustrate me

Single mommas watch your coins and your finances.

Central Focus: Child support can be a terrible situation to discuss, but you will have to discuss your finances and get creative!

(Even when your child support is $1.00...that's right, ten dimes/100 pennies.)

Yes, my ex-husband gave our son $1.00 for child support one time. Honey, I wanted superpowers that day so that I could chop him in the back of his neck and then fly away. lol.

You have to get creative with your finances and make provisions for your family. Guess what?! Ain't no sugar daddy nor is Hakim from Empire going to show up and rescue your family.

So get to work mommas, you have to get out of your own way. Create a company, sell dinners, bake cookies. We sold candy and created care packages. You know the shampoo and conditioner from the hotels? I would repackage them and sell those to the high schoolers. Let's just say they didn't smell too fresh after gym and I saw an opportunity to provide for my children.

My family struggled to make ends meet. I quickly turned that Struggle Shit into a Survivor Situation. "I'm A Survivor. I'm not gonna give up!

Sing that as you get creative.

Don't let someone who gave up on their dreams talk you out of yours!

Affirmations:

I affirm to be a survivor

I affirm to create a small business

I affirm to focus on the positive

* All you need is an idea and serious drive. Our kids are the reason to seek out a better life

Single mommas, be the friend you want in your ex-relationship, divorced relationship, baby daddy or baby mama situation.

<u>Central Focus:</u> I know this ain't easy.

Creating an environment of forgiveness for your family means that ultimately someone has to be the bigger person.   Now mommas listen to me; this process will take a whole lot of time praying, a whole LOT OF JESUS and hard work. However, your children will thank you later.

Let me slide on over here and do the stanky leg and say this, I know some of you are probably saying what if I don't want to be the friend, well hell, DROP THE MIC like OBAMA and be out!

Forgiveness is a process, and you will need a whole lot of JESUS to get you to that point.

Affirmations:

I affirm to look for inspiration in everything

I affirm to take control of my life

I affirm to awaken my confidence

Single mommas create A I Need Help Day.

Central Focus: As single mothers, we struggle with asking for help. We will eff things up in the worst way before we seek any support. Recognize that you might not have it all figured out right now, and it's ok to call for help.

Support can be the neighbor, coaches, teachers, guidance counselors or church members. Make sure you get a background check on these folks...I'm just saying.

Affirmations:

I affirm to seek help when I'm feeling overwhelmed

I affirm to surround my self with positive relationships

I affirm to prioritize my health and well-being

#21

Single mommas have a Hell Naw Section inside the house.

Central Focus: As a mother, we do everything in our power to facilitate everything right. It's our job to set the standards for a relationship with dad, teachers, coaches, sports, assisting with prom outfits. The fun begins when you start missing the lotion around the house...HA! And that's when you will have to have the dreading conversation about the birds and the bees.

Let me explain this when I had to have the conversation about the birds in the bees. I was clueless about how to address the conversation. The truth is that I really didn't want to discuss this topic.

That's how we came up with the Hell Naw night, suggestions box and Hell Naw this is how I'm feeling at this moment.

In short, create a section in your home where your family can deposit their Hell Naw moments and be free.

Trust me; kids have **Hell Naw** moments that they want to express as well.

They may want to vent to you directly about the absent parent, school, sports or the nagging mother you have become.

When your children grow comfortable and begin opening up during Hell Naw Night, make sure you leave all your judging out. Welcome the conversation and never be **vengeful.** Children may discuss that they may feel inadequate, worried, rejected, afraid, lonely and even discouraged. **Be open-minded, be involved in how they may feel**.

Affirmations:

I affirm that I am enough

I affirm that God loves me

I affirm that every feeling that I have, God has a scripture for me to relinquish my feelings.

Breakthrough Moment that gives you the facts you need to make important decisions.

Hurt- Psalm 34:18

Feel inadequate- Psalms 139:14

I feel rejected -Psalm 31:16

I feel afraid – Psalm 91:4

I'm lonely – Hebrews 13:5

#22

Single mommas talk to your children.

Central Focus: Allow them to have a suggestion box/improvement box in the home.

Accept the fact that your children have feelings. And for them to grow, we need to have a loving and caring environment that consists of creativity, laughter, love, and spirituality.

Affirmations:

I affirm to be kind to my family feelings

I affirm to surround my family with love, laughter, and loyalty

I affirm to help my family tap into their inner strength

Single mommas teach your kids how to Enjoy the Moment!

Central Focus: To look at your children or child greatest gifts and become their cheerleader and biggest fan.

Heck Look at me, I have three boys, one king of the jungle, The Real TaRzann, one sex in the city basketball playing, lip-smacking, L.L Cool J cool ass type college kid and the last is the beast mode sports kid, who eats every two hours and was diagnosed with multiple disabilities.

Shit if my shame the devil. This should show you how I have broken the stereotype of a single family household.

We are raising our families in a world of instant gratification. Teach your family that you have to enjoy the current moment. Embrace the possibilities, do less, and stop worrying about the future.

Be mindful and remain fully present. Enjoy the simple things with your family, like homework and time with friends and family because this goes by so fast. You'll wonder how and where did the time go!! This is the only way to enjoy life to the fullest and stay current. It will take some time and practice. However, it is achievable.

———————————

Affirmations:

I affirm to put the cell phone down when I'm with my family

I affirm to be present when my family requires my attention

I affirm to support my family with all of their dreams and goals

#24

Single mommas read your bible and create an intimate relationship with God.

<u>Central Focus</u>: You can talk to God just as if you are talking to your Girls. You know those intimate conversation we have how we are building a perfect man and we give details down to his biceps, his lips and how he should walk. My love, that's how you have to talk to God. Let him know your heart desires and be detailed with everything you want God to bless you with. Let me give an example "Lord I desire to have an intimate relationship with you. I want my relationship to be on fleek with you God that it falls out of my skins. I want my faith to be like the platinum card." You get my drift something like that. Now that how you have a real conversation with God.

And, you won't go to hell if you read the bible with a glass of wine, red lipstick, and a cute pair of jeans...girl you see I'm still living. Be a radical saint with your blemishes. God will fix all of your broken pieces. We are all a work in progress; I know the bible says come as you are, so show up!

Give yourself permission to have access to spiritual education, read as much as you can, self- improve and be a Happy Mother.

It doesn't matter what's going on around you.

What matters is what's going on inside of your heart.

Affirmation:

I affirm to have a healthy relationship with GOD

I affirm to have unshakeable faith

I affirm to honor and value myself

Kick-Ass Single Mom: 24 Strategies Notes

WHAT I HAVE LEARNED

AS A KICK SINGLE A$$ MOM..

As a single mother, you are going to have to make choices. I made the very decision to narrow my life story down to helping other woman deal with their circumstances surrounding single parenting.

You will have to be committed.
I mean firm about your commitment to single parenting

FOCUS: 5 VITAL STEPS TO SINGLE PARENTING

1. Taking Single Parenting One Day At A Time..

2. Be A Positive Parent.

3. Be A Parent that is willing to listen.

4. Be willing to be unapologetic about your family status.

5. Be willing to sit still and listen to GOD's direction for your Family and then take actions.

Central Focus: *SPEAKING LIFE OVER YOURSELF DAILY*

I AM ABLE…. PHIL 4:13

I AM STRONG … ISIAH 41.10

I AM COURAGEOUS…. DEUT 31.6

What You Have Learned

AS A KICK SINGLE A$$ MOM..

_____
_____
_____
_____
_____
_____
_____
_____
_____
_____
_____
_____
_____
_____
_____
_____
_____
_____
_____
_____
_____
_____
_____
_____
_____
_____
_____
_____

Latiqua 11 Commandments

*The Most Valuable thing you can pass onto your love
ones are
Commandments that will last forever*

Latiqua Williams

Latiqua's 11 Commandments

1. Thou shall put God first in your life and family.
    (Matthew 6:33)

    Be fun, laugh, joke and rejoice.

2. Thou shall not give a dang what others think.
   (Proverbs 29:25)

3. Thou shall love thy self inside and out.
   (Philippians 2:15)

4. Thou shall work hard & play harder. Man doesn't work; man doesn't eat.
   (2 Thessalonians 3:10)

5. Thou shall not compare children or families.

   They are all different; they grow up different.
   (2 Corinthians 10:12)

6. Thou shall change your mindset.

You can improve your situation whenever you get ready.
(Romans 12:2)

7. Thou shall shut the door to fear.

Lord help me to recognize the presence of fear.
(2 Timothy 1:7)

8. Thou shall not say why me. But try me!
(Isaiah 55 8:9)

9.   Thou shall have a clean heart.

Create a clean heart- renew my spirit and mind.
(Psalm 51:10)

10. Thou shall seek wisdom for life.

Girl, I can't depend on my common sense. I need GOD's sense.

Ask for daily wisdom.
(Proverbs 3:16)

11. Thou shall forgive self and others. Mommas believe in your potential, not your past.
(Acts 13:38)

These 11 Commandments will provide you with guidance in learning the circumstances of single parenting. Providing you with daily wisdom when you become frustrated and for the days you wake up feeling emotional.

As a mother, you have to know who you are, what your building and birthing. I urge you to use these commandments for your family needs and getting you through the day.

Always Remember:
"I am building a house where the floors are made of up strength, Where the walls are crafted of ambition, and Where the roof is a masterpiece of forgiveness."
- Woor Unnahar

Kick-Ass Single Mom Cheat Sheet

When you write your cheat sheet, please grab your best **HIGH HEELS** and your Favorite **LIPSTICK**.

Keep in mind; you are about to write about your family boundaries, negotiation plan, bonus parenting, breaking generational curses, deceased parents, boo-boo kitty.

Every healthy relationship needs boundaries to keep things in perspective.

For example, in my family, we do not focus on generation bondage or the stereotypes of society that says African American Males can't be raised successfully by single African American Women.

Our family is a product of prayer, power, and action! I was determined that my three sons would be part of the 3C's in Life! The **CHOICE** to make a difference, the choice to take a **CHANCE** and I knew our life would **CHANGE**. By establishing what is permissible and what is not within our family boundaries allows us to protect our family.

Boundaries you may need to set in your family relationship may vary, but the reason for establishing them remains the same. Keeping negative situation and people away from your family and protecting what's within your family relationship is important.

I will admit setting Family boundaries and saying no to people, or family members may not be the easiest. However, it is necessary.

I recall a time during my divorce when we had to arrange a visitation schedule for my youngest son, setting my family boundaries for my ex-husband was no easy task. The schedule he was requesting was not realistic and I knew in my heart he would not be able to keep up with what he was asking. So I made the decision to divide the week visitation schedule that would allow us to have amicable time with our son.

Well, let's just say that schedule worked for about a good 2-months or so.

The first real improvement came when I decided that I would not allow my sons feeling be on an emotional roller coaster ride. So I made a sound decision to Repent for any unresolved feelings that I had about my ex-husband. Stopped blaming him for his lack of commitment and made a choice to declare that I will no longer blame him. I will implement boundaries so my son will have a healthy lifestyle. No more struggling with the Why or the what's of disappointment.

No Headaches, No fussing.. All you do is Set Boundaries you will discover how easy it is to facilitate a step –by-step no-nonsense lifestyle

Trust me it can be trying as a single parent and overwhelming at times. Simply confess daily to God that you trust him to supply all your needs: Spiritual, financial, physical.

Your Family is not a statistic or a number in the poverty system.

Your family is tailored made by **GOD** with gifts and abilities that will be displayed in the world.

A mother who will never give up on her family, always remember that you are the voice for your family.

1 Corinthians 10:13

Says He Will not put on me no more than I can bear

Lets Kick Ass and Write

No Holding Back!

Now lets break this word down.

- *I am A-anointed*
- *I am S- saved*
- *I am S- still standing as a single Parent*

Healthy family boundaries are limits and rules that we place for families and ourselves. What is acceptable and what is not, in single-parent homes your boundaries can vary. Such as thoughts and ideas. The honest truth is you can place emotional boundaries, time boundaries, physical boundaries and even material boundaries within your healthy family.

It's time for action write out what your healthy family boundaries are

_____

_____

_____

_____

You be the judge of what's appropriate, and what's not appropriate your family

_____

_____

_____

_____

What is the perfect reflection of your healthy family goals

_____

_____

_____

_____

Don't settle for anything less

_____

_____

_____

_____

_____

Build your family confidence and write a Healthy Family Affirmation:

_____

_____

_____

_____

_____

Family Non-Negotiable – A family boundary that is simply not open for discussion or modification. To be perfectly honest, I allowed myself to be in a relationship many years later that I knew dang on well was on my family non- negotiable list. The final results was that I had to love myself enough to look in the mirror and say goodbye to the unhealthy relationship… Never again will I modify my life for any unpractical relationships.

The way I look at it, even children should be allowed to have non-negotiable.

What's your family Non-Negotiable?

_____

_____

_____

_____

_____

_____

_____

_____

_____

Create your family Non –Negotiable Affirmation:

_____

_____

_____

_____

_____

_____

_____

_____

_____

What is Boo- Boo Kitty allowed to do with the kids ..

You've probably noticed earlier in the book I mentioned Boo- Boo Kitty.. Let me be honest I wish this was what ran across my mind when raising my kids. **Boo- boo** kitty is simple your ex-man new girlfriend; she is not yet qualified to be stepmother title because they are not legally married.

It's hard enough to parent without having to worry about boo- boo kitty. The truth is, it took me a very long time and some maturing before I wrote this sheet out. Here are just a few of what Boo-Boo kitty was allowed to be a part of.

1. If absent parent dated more than 30 days, she would be allowed to events
2. I requested that adults would meet and discuss the best interest of my child. (We all had to leave out our negative thoughts of each other) let's just say some days were better than others.

What I'm leading up to is this once you write out what's allowed for boo-boo kitty this gives you the power to move forward in life. You have total control

What is Boo-Boo Kitty allowed to do with the kids while you and your ex is co-parenting?

_____

_____

_____

_____

_____

How will you adapt your BBK LIST (boo-boo kitty list) to fit your specific needs for the child /or children?

_____

_____

_____

_____

_____

Create your healthy Affirmation:

_____

_____

_____

_____

_____

_____

_____

_____

The last three pages are simply powerful strategies for taking charge of your single parent life. It's a turbocharge straight talk about family boundaries, non-negotiable, boo-boo kitty and parenting with confidence. Maybe one of the topics we discussed offset some emotional triggers or a mixture of feelings and you may have even decided to come back to this section of the book.

No problem!

Trust me it's completely fine. Come to think of it, when I was writing out my **family boundaries, BBK list (boo-boo kitty)** and my **non-negotiable**. I broke out in hives as I was writing, instantly a headache came, everything that could have distracted me did.

Until I was like Sister Girl Obviously you need some self –cleaning.

I had to say goodbye to the headaches, the damn rash that only showed when I wanted to take charge of my life. In the privacy of my home I locked myself in the bathroom, I knew nobody would bother me. Allowing my self to look in the mirror and cry!!! I pulled no punches, uncovering and unmasking facts about what I really wanted for my family. INSTEAD of weeks in no time, I was writing with ease.

There's simply no substitute for what you may feel when you're demanding a lifestyle facelift. Take a minute or to ease your mind and tap into your inner strength. The good news is you decide at your own pace how you facelift your life.

Let me emphasize transformation is a daily process and It's important that you endure the journey. Endure and enjoy the journey; today is the day to relinquish anything that will keep you from enjoying this journey in life.

Journey Affirmation: I am a woman who is on a journey to shine her light bright and live out her passion and purpose in life.

"I am fearfully and wonderfully made "– Psalm 139: 1:14

I Break Stereotypes Not People ..

Dear Single Mother,

I want you to starve your fear and feed your faith. Today choose to take off the cape of fear, no more allowing insecurities that you may have about single parenting limit you. Say good riddance to False Evidence Appearing Raising A Family. (FEAR)

How we feel in our minds impact how we feel in our bodies. Stimulate your body, mind, and soul with positive thoughts and affirmation.

Repeat this affirmation after each sheet you complete.

Affirm: God, I want you to squeeze all of the insecurities as a single parent out of me RIGHT NOW!

I want you to FILL ME with love, guidance, and wisdom on this journey as a single parent.

I don't have it all figured out, and I don't have all the answer. But I know you do GOD. You can provide me the strength to do this job as a Single Mother.

I fully surrender to you!

Please continue to provide me with insight, wisdom to be the best single parent.

"For God hath not given us the spirit of fear but of power, and love and a sound mind." 2 Timothy 1:7

I Break Stereotypes Not People

I think you'll be shocked by what you're about to read about the single mother Stereotypes

Stereotypes – A widely held but a fixed and oversimplified image or idea of a particular type of person or thing. (Oxford dictionary definition)

Prepare yourself for two shocking myths,

1. **MYTH**: Single mothers are portrayed as struggling mothers who only receive public assistance
2. **MYTH**: Single Mothers are LOUD and Rude

   Ok, I'm done, for some reason, this topic gives me a headache. Because this is some bull... I must say that I wholeheartedly disagree with both of these Myths..

Not all single parents are loud and rude, we all come from different walks of life. Until you have witnessed or walked a mile in a single mother shoes, I say throw those myths in the trash.

Single mothers, like myself, maintain successful jobs and do a damn good job raising our families. Now I want to make one thing very clear, during my divorce I went through a period were my family and I went through a hard time and we were on public assistance for a short period of time. Not once did I allow anything or anyone to portray my family as what is listed above.

I simply kept this engraved into my mind never underestimate the power of a single mother.

I'm just gonna simply say.. A black single mother at that which is on a mission to raise her family bold and confident..

Define I Break Stereotypes for your family....

What Stereotypes are you willing to break?

_____

_____

_____

_____

_____

_____

_____

_____

_____

_____

_____

_____

_____

_____

_____

_____

_____

_____

_____

_____

_____

_____

_____

_____

_____

Single Mothers Family Prayer

I Pray on this day that God arms me with vital insights on single motherhood.

I Pray on this day God that you provide me with wisdom, clarity, and peace.

I Pray on this day God that my children or child is shielding with your protection

I Pray on this day God that you provide me with a sense of patience and understanding.

I Pray on this day God that you expand my knowledge as a single mother.

I Pray on this day God that you stretch my mind

I Pray on this day God that you give me the spirit to make important decisions

I Pray on this day God that you will guide my family in the right direction

My Prayer is that you find the strength to be A Kick A$$ Single Mom…

Ask and it will be given to you,

Seek, and you will find,

Knock, and it will be opened to You..

Matthew 7:7

Kick Ass Single Mom

Congratulations, you made it!   You now have the tools
to what I define as being a
KICK ASS SINGLE MOM!

I hope it was an enjoyable read and that you found it to
be motivating and inspiring!

Now, I challenge you to not let this be a passive read.

Instead, make it an active one! Take charge of your life
because you can do it!

With love, from a mother who had to own her mess!
A mother who was crippled with Fear.
A mother who fought for her family.
A mother who kicked her way beyond the stereotypes.

So, I ask you today as you have experienced a part of my
life, what is holding you back from telling your story?
Incredible things happen when you allow God to
use you the way you are.

Can I just say..........

You are the BOMB.com single mama, mom, bonus, boo-boo kitty!!!!! Whatever your title maybe You are a woman that can raise a successful family. You are a woman that knows how to **KEEP** it real and set boundaries for yourself and loves one....... and simply tell your self all day every day .. **I AM THE BEST!!**

Conference / Summit / Seminar / Speaking Engagement / Training

Pity to Powerful

I'm raising Successful sons with Jesus

Learn how to faith it Forward without filters

The P FACTORS (PRAY PUSH PURPOSE)

Change thy Mindset

Beauty Brows Business

How to forgive your Past

The Radical single mom who loves Jesus with heels

I'm Saved with Red Lipstick Now WHAT!

I AM ENOUGH

Self-Love

Self Confidence

Discover, live and thrive in your life's TRUE PURPOSE

Take Action

Stimulate Your Mind

Educational

Learn how to Create from where you Are

Hair loss Restoration

Beauty & Biz Classes

Empowering women Through Hair Loss

Teaching women how to build their own beauty empire in Hair Loss

How to start your own Hair Care Company

Look Out for Other Titles

Single Moms in Heel's manual workbook & other Chapters

Pity To Powerful

Pity To Powerful Manual

Moms Guide To Starting A Business On A Budget

Faith It Forward With No Filter

A Sister Guide to Homeschooling African American Sons

Jesus Love You with Your Blemishes

Hair Restoration Guide For Beauty Professionals

How To Slay In Hair Loss

Inspirational Manual For Abused to Abundantly Woman

Meet the Author

Latiqua Williams is best known for educating, motivating and stimulating your mind about creating a lifestyle that turns your pity mindset into a dominant one. Her goal is to create a community of influential women to inspire them to embrace their inner beauty as mothers, entrepreneurs or whatever God has empowered her to be.

A Kick Ass Woman Willing to Break Stereotypes!

www.Latiquawilliams.com
Instagram-latiqua_williams
Facebook: Latiqua Williams The Stimulator
FacebookGroup: Brilliance Beyond Beauty Sisterhood
Podcast: She Did It In Heels

You have the keys to unlock your Power

www.ingramcontent.com/pod-product-compliance
Lightning Source LLC
Chambersburg PA
CBHW062353090426
42740CB00036B/2402